Planning for Learning through Opposites

by Judith Harries. Illustrated by Cathy Hughes

Contents

Making plans 2-3

Using the 'Early Learning Goals' 4-6

EYFS Planning Chart 7

Theme 1: Happy and sad 8-9

Theme 2: Big and small 10-11

Theme 3: Old and new 12-13

Theme 4: Hot and cold 14-15

Theme 5: Loud and quiet 16-17

Theme 6: Up and down 18-19

Bringing it all together – 'Pyjama Party' 20

Resources 21

Collecting evidence of children's learning 22

Activity overview 23

Home links 24

Family page Inside back cover

Published by Practical Pre-School Books, A Division of MA Education Ltd,
St Jude's Church, Dulwich Road, Herne Hill, London, SE24 0PB Tel: 020 7738 5454
www.practicalpreschoolbooks.com

Revised edition (2nd edition) © MA Education Ltd 2014. First edition © MA Education Limited 2010.
Front cover image © iStockphoto.com/fishwork. Back cover images (left-right) Lucie Carlier © MA Education Ltd, Ben Suri © MA Education Ltd.

All rights reserved. No part of this publication may be reproduced, stored in a retrieval system, or transmitted
by any means, electronic, mechanical, photocopied or otherwise, without the prior permission of the publisher.

Planning for Learning through Opposites ISBN: 978-1-909280-67-0

Making plans

Child-friendly planning

The purpose of planning is to make sure that all children enjoy a broad and balanced experience of learning. Planning should be flexible, useful and child-friendly. It should reflect opportunities available both indoors and outside. Plans form part of a planning cycle in which practitioners make observations, assess and plan.

Children benefit from reflective planning that takes into account the children's current interests and abilities and also allows them to take the next steps in their learning. Plans should make provision for activity that promotes learning and a desire to imagine, observe, communicate, experiment, investigate and create.

Plans should include a variety of types of activity. Some will be adult-initiated or adult-led, that focus on key skills or concepts. These should be balanced with opportunities for child-initiated activity where the children take a key role in the planning. In addition there is a need to plan for the on-going continuous provision areas such as construction, sand and water, malleable materials, small world, listening area, role-play and mark-making. Thought also needs to be given to the enhanced provision whereby an extra resource or change may enable further exploration, development and learning.

The outdoor environment provides valuable opportunities for children's learning. It is vital that plans value the use of outdoor space.

The UK Frameworks

Within the UK a number of frameworks exist to outline the provision that children should be entitled to receive. Whilst a variety of terms and labels are used to describe the Areas of Learning there are key principles which are common to each document. For example they advocate that practitioners' planning should be personal based on observations and knowledge of the specific children within a setting. They acknowledge that young children learn best when there is scope for child-initiated activity. In addition it is accepted that young children's learning is holistic. Although within the documents Areas of Learning are presented separately to ensure that key areas are not over-looked, within settings, children's learning will combine areas. Thus the Areas of Learning are perhaps of most use for planning, assessment and recording.

Focused area plans

The plans you make for each day will outline areas of continuous provision and focused, adult-led activities. Plans for focused-area activities need to include aspects such as:

- resources needed;
- the way in which you might introduce activities;
- individual needs;
- the organisation of adult help;
- size of the group;
- timing;
- safety;
- key vocabulary.

Identify the learning and the Early Learning Goals that each activity is intended to promote. Make a note of any assessments or observations that you are likely to carry out. After carrying out the activities, make notes on your plans to say what was particularly successful, or any changes you would make another time.

A final note

Planning should be seen as flexible. Not all groups meet every day, and not all children attend every day. Any part of the plan can be used independently, stretched over a longer period or condensed to meet the needs of any group. You will almost certainly adapt the activities as children respond to them in different ways and bring their own ideas, interests and enthusiasms. The important thing is to ensure that the

Making plans

children are provided with a varied and enjoyable curriculum that meets their individual developing needs.

Using the book

Read the section which outlines links to the Early Learning Goals (pages 4-6) and explains the rationale for focusing on 'Opposites'.

The chart on page 7 gives an example format for weekly planning. It provides opportunity to plan for the on-going continuous provision, as well as more focused activities.

Use pages 8 to 19 to select from a wide range of themed, focused activities that recognise the importance of involving children in practical activities and giving them opportunities to follow their own interests. For each 'Opposites' theme, two activities are described in detail as examples to help you in your planning and preparation. Key vocabulary, questions and learning opportunities are identified. Use the activities as a basis to:

- extend current and emerging interests and capabilities
- engage in sustained conversations
- stimulate new interests and skills.

Find out on page 20 how the 'Opposites' activities can be brought together with the 'Pyjama Party' and 'Opposites Parade'.

Use page 21 for ideas of resources to collect or prepare. Remember that the books listed are only suggestions. It is likely that you will already have within your setting a variety of other books that will be equally useful.

The activity overview chart on page 23 can be used either at the planning stage or after each theme has been completed. It will help you to see at a glance which aspects of children's development are being addressed and alert you to the areas which may need greater input in the future.

As children take part in the activities, their learning will progress. 'Collecting evidence' on page 22 explains how you might monitor each child's achievements.

There is additional material to support the working partnership of families and children in the form of a reproducible Family page found inside the back cover.

It is important to appreciate that the ideas presented in this book will only be a part of your planning. Many activities that will be taking place as routine in your group may not be mentioned. For example, it is assumed that sand, dough, water, puzzles, role play, floor toys, technology and large scale apparatus are part of the ongoing early years experience. Role-play areas, stories, rhymes, singing, and group discussion times are similarly assumed to be happening in each week although they may not be a focus for described activities.

Using the 'Early Learning Goals'

The principles that are common to each of the United Kingdom curriculum frameworks for the early years are described on page 2. It is vital that, when planning for children within a setting, practitioners are familiar with the relevant framework's content and organisation for areas of learning. Regardless however, of whether a child attends a setting in England, Northern Ireland, Scotland or Wales they have a right to provision for all areas of learning. The children should experience activities which encourage them to develop their communication and language; personal, social, emotional, physical, mathematical and creative skills. They should have opportunities within literacy and be encouraged to understand and explore their world.

Within the Statutory Framework for the Early Years Foundation Stage (2012), Communication and Language; Physical Development and Personal, Social and Emotional Development are described as Prime Areas of Learning that are 'particularly crucial for igniting children's curiosity and enthusiasm for learning, and for building their capacity to learn, form relationships and thrive' (page 4, DfE 2012). The Specific Areas of Learning are Literacy, Mathematics, Understanding the World and Expressive Arts and Design.

For each Area of Learning the Early Learning Goals (ELGs) describe what children are expected to be able to do by the time they enter Year 1. These goals, detailed on pages 4 to 6, have been used throughout this book to show how activities relating to 'Opposites' could link to these expectations. For example, for Personal, Social and Emotional Development, one aim relates to the development of children's 'self-confidence and self-awareness'. Activities suggested which provide the opportunity for children to do this have the reference PSE1. This will enable you to see which parts of the Early Learning Goals are covered for a given theme and to plan for areas to be revisited and developed.

In addition, an activity may be carried out to develop a range of different Early Learning Goals. For example, when the children write invitations for Grandparent's Day they will develop their writing skills for Literacy. Also, when they write with a pencil and illlustrate their concertina books, they will use their fine motor skills which are part of Physical Development. Thus, whilst adult-focused activities may have clearly defined goals at the planning stage, it must be remembered that as children take on ideas and initiate their own learning and activities, goals may change.

The Prime Areas of Learning
Communication and Language

Listening and attention: children listen attentively in a range of situations. They listen to stories, accurately anticipating key events and respond to what they hear with relevant comments, questions or actions. They give their attention to what others say and respond appropriately, while engaged in another activity. (CL1)

Understanding: children follow instructions involving several ideas or actions. They answer 'how' and 'why' questions about their experiences and in response to stories or events. (CL2)

Speaking: children express themselves effectively, showing awareness of listeners' needs. They use past, present and future forms accurately when talking about events that have happened or are to happen in the future. They develop their own narratives and explanations by connecting ideas or events. (CL3)

'Opposites' provides many opportunities for children to enjoy listening, understanding and speaking. There are a wide range of books featuring 'Opposites' and these can be used to stimulate interest in the chosen themes, encouraging children to listen and to talk. When discussing opposite moods and talking about hot and cold activities, children will have the opportunity to ask questions. Setting up and using role-play areas such as the Bear cave will allow the children to follow instructions and develop their own narratives. Playing 'I went to the shop and bought a new...', and making up stories about Loud Luke and Quiet Queenie for others to listen to, will encourage children to express themselves and to show awareness of listeners' needs.

Physical Development

Moving and handling: children show good control and co-ordination in large and small movements. They move confidently in a range of ways, safely negotiating space. They handle equipment and tools effectively, including pencils for writing. (PD1)

Health and self-care: children know the importance for good health of physical exercise, and a healthy diet, and talk about ways to keep healthy and safe. They manage their own basic hygiene and personal needs successfully, including dressing and going to the toilet independently. (PD2)

The topic of 'Opposites' offers many opportunities for children to enjoy movement activities and to handle tools and equipment. When children make big and small junk models, play traditional circle and other movement games, dance the 'Opposites Dance' and pretend to be 'Jack in the boxes', they can develop and demonstrate control and co-ordination. Throwing bean bags, using big and small hoops, making pop-up puppets, and using play dough to make long and short snakes, will allow children to use small equipment and promote the development of fine motor skills. In addition, any of the described literacy activities where children write will also contribute to the development of 'handling' skills. Children will practise dressing skills on their teddy bears and understand the importance of physical exercise through the warm up exercises. Areas such as basic hygiene and going to the toilet independently, however, will be part of on-going, daily activity.

Personal, Social and Emotional Development

Self-confidence and self-awareness: children are confident to try new activities, and say why they like some activities more than others. They are confident to speak in a familiar group, will talk about their ideas, and will choose the resources they need for their chosen activities. They say when they do or don't need help. (PSE1)

Managing feelings and behaviour: children talk about how they and others show feelings, talk about their own and others' behaviour, and its consequences, and know that some behaviour is unacceptable. They work as part of a group or class, and understand and follow the rules. They adjust their behaviour to different situations, and take changes of routine in their stride. (PSE2)

Making relationships: children play co-operatively, taking turns with others. They take account of one another's ideas about how to organise their activity. They show sensitivity to others' needs and feelings, and form positive relationships with adults and other children. (PSE3)

'Opposites' offer many opportunities, both for child-initiated and adult-led activities, which will develop children personally, socially and emotionally. Considering the need to say 'please' and 'thank you' when their Grandparents visit the setting, going out on an 'Opposites hunt', and playing games together such as Snakes and ladders gives children the opportunity to consider acceptable behaviour. Collaborating to play 'Mirrors' and 'Chinese whispers', some parachute games and planning the 'Pyjama Party' will encourage children to make relationships. Many of the areas described within the ELGs for Personal, Social and Emotional Development though, will be covered on an almost incidental basis. Any activity that involves making choices, or showing initiative, will promote self-confidence and self-awareness.

The Specific Areas of Learning
Literacy

Reading: children read and understand simple sentences. They use phonic knowledge to decode regular words and read them aloud accurately. They also read some common irregular words. They demonstrate understanding when talking with others about what they have read. (L1)

Writing: children use their phonic knowledge to write words in ways which match their spoken sounds. They also write some irregular common words. They write simple sentences which can be read by themselves and others. Some words are spelt correctly and others are phonetically plausible. (L2)

Activities for 'Opposites', based on picture books and stories, will provide opportunities for the children to read using both their phonic knowledge and memories of common, irregular words. Discussions of the stories will help children to understand and to develop their vocabularies. Activities such as making a name-string, writing a concertina story book, making invitations, and creating hot and cold poems will encourage children to explore the sounds within words and to enjoy the early stages of writing.

Mathematics

Numbers: children count reliably with numbers from 1 to 20, place them in order and say which number is one more or one less than a given number. Using quantities and objects, they add and subtract two single-digit numbers and count on or back to find the answer. They solve problems, including doubling, halving and sharing. (M1)

Shape, space and measures: children use everyday language to talk about size, weight, capacity, position, distance, time and money to compare quantities and objects and to solve problems. They recognise, create and describe patterns. They explore characteristics of everyday objects and shapes and use mathematical language to describe them. (M2)

Activities for 'Opposites' provide many opportunities for children to count, to measure and to explore shape and space.

Using the Fish finger rhyme, counting candles in play dough birthday cakes and writing a chart of favourite drinks encourage children to count and to compare. Making shape collages of happy and sad faces, threading beads in patterns, and creating loud and quiet musical patterns helps the children to develop awareness of shape and pattern. Measuring using hands, weighing boxes, and investigating capacity in the sand and water trays increases children's awareness of sizes and measurements.

Understanding the World

People and communities: children talk about past and present events in their own lives and in the lives of family members. They know that other children don't always enjoy the same things, and are sensitive to this. They know about similarities and differences between themselves and others, and among families, communities and traditions. (UW1)

The world: children know about similarities and differences in relation to places, objects, materials and living things. They talk about the features of their own immediate environment and how environments might vary from one another. They make observations of animals and plants and explain why some things occur, and talk about changes. (UW2)

Technology: children recognise that a range of technology is used in places such as homes and schools. They select and use technology for particular purposes. (UW3)

To understand their world, children need times to gain knowledge, explore and relate what they discover to both previously held ideas and future learning. When looking at life in hot and cold countries, baking scones, making jelly and conducting experiments with ice cubes, children will be able to make comparisons and notice similarities and differences. Investigating floating and sinking, and looking at how musical instruments work encourages children to investigate and ask questions. When children take photographs of happy and sad faces, they have the opportunity to use technology. Technology will also feature in role-play as well as being part of the on-going, daily provision. Discussions with parents and grandparents about family trees and how games, toys and clothes have changed will provide opportunity to consider events from the past, the present and the future.

Expressive Arts and Design

Exploring and using media and materials: children sing songs, make music and dance, and experiment with ways of changing them. They safely use and explore a variety of materials, tools and techniques, experimenting with colour, design, texture, form and function. (EAD1)

Being imaginative: children use what they have learnt about media and materials in original ways, thinking about uses and purposes. They represent their own ideas, thoughts and feelings through design and technology, art, music, dance, role-play and stories. (EAD2)

Whilst involved in activities for 'Opposites', children will experience working with a variety of materials, tools and techniques as they paint happy and sad portraits, big and little pictures, make hot and cold collages and design press tile patterns. When doing actions and using percussion during the singing of songs that feature Opposites, children have the chance to be imaginative. Throughout all the activities children should be encouraged to talk about what they see and feel as they communicate their ideas in painting, model making, music and role play.

Note

The Early Learning Goals raise awareness of key aspects within any child's development for each Area of Learning. It is important to remember that these goals are reached through a combination of adult and child-initiated activity within Early Years settings and also a child's home life. Thus, it is vital that goals are shared by practitioners and parents, and children are given every opportunity to develop throughout their Early Years Foundation Stage at home and within a setting.

Example chart to aid planning in the EYFS

Week beginning:	Monday	Tuesday	Wednesday	Thursday	Friday
FOCUSED ACTIVITIES					
Focus Activity 1:					
Focus Activity 2:					
Stories and rhymes					
CONTINUOUS PROVISION (Indoor)					
Collage					
Construction (large)					
Construction (small)					
ICT					
Imaginative play					
Listening					
Malleable materials					
Mark making					
Painting					
Role play					
Sand (damp)					
Sand (dry)					
Water					
CONTINUOUS PROVISION (Outdoor)					
Construction					
Creative play					
Exploratory play					
Gross motor					
ENHANCED PROVISION (Indoor)					
ENHANCED PROVISION (Outdoor)					

Planning for Learning through Opposites

Theme 1: Happy and sad

Communication and Language
- Make a class book of 'Opposites' beginning with 'happy and sad' and add to it throughout the topic. Ask children to draw or cut out pictures of happy and sad faces. Can they make up stories about why the faces look happy or sad? Film or record the children telling their stories. Scribe them into the book. (CL1, 2)
- Open an 'Opposites corner' for children to sit in. Make a collection of Opposites books (see Resources), toys, games and puzzles. (CL1)

Physical Development
- Play 'Throw that feeling'. Sit in a circle and throw a beanbag to a child. Ask them to show you a feeling with their face. Then repeat with a different feeling. (PD1)
- Make happy and sad mobiles from salt dough (see activity opposite). (PD1)
- Play 'Happy and sad'. Ask the children to dance around with smiley faces when they hear the music. When it stops they must stand still and look sad. (PD1)
- Make happy and sad pop-up puppets. Provide wooden spoons and help children to paint a happy face on one side and a sad one on the other. Decorate short cardboard tubes and make the puppets pop up. (PD1)

Personal, Social and Emotional Development
- Introduce the theme by talking about the word 'opposite'. Play a circle game (see activity opposite). (PSE3)
- During circle time, encourage children to pull happy and sad faces. Pass round a mirror so they can look at their expressions. Ask children what makes them feel happy or sad. Pass a smile around the circle. (PSE1, 2)
- Play 'Mirrors'. Ask children to sit facing a partner and copy every move they make. Try 'Mirror opposites' – if your partner smiles, you must look sad. (PSE3)
- Read *Happy Hippo, Angry Duck* by Sandra Boynton. Talk about different moods and feelings. Can the children talk about some opposite moods such as happy and sad, angry and calm, and so on? (PSE2)
- Read *Dogger* by Shirley Hughes. How do the children feel when they lose a special toy? (PSE2)

Literacy
- Make a list of opposite words. Write and illustrate them onto pre-cut star shapes and display in the Opposites corner as a wall chart. (L1, 2)
- Ask the children if they can tell you any funny jokes or stories. Write them into a joke book to help make people smile.

Mathematics
- Use pre-cut sticky paper shapes to make happy and sad faces. Ask children to name the shapes they have chosen. (M2)
- Enjoy using this food rhyme:
  Five fish fingers, for your tea.
  Will you share just one with me?
  Eating one will make me glad.
  There's four left, please don't be sad.
  Four fish fingers...
  Change the food type. (M1)

Understanding the World
- Help children to take photographs of each other looking happy and sad. (UW3)
- In the 'Opposites corner', display pictures of countries in the world that are 'opposite' – such as hot and cold, North and South, big and small, and so on. (UW2)

Expressive Arts and Design
- Sing the 'Opposites' song from Bingo Lingo (see Resources). (EAD1)
- Sing 'If you're happy and you know it, clap your hands'. Sing it slowly and change to 'If you're sad and you know it, look like this' and pull sad faces. (EAD1)
- Ask children to paint happy and sad self-portraits. Use hand mirrors to look at faces. Label with captions to explain why the faces are happy or sad (EAD1)
- Use paper plates to make happy and sad masks. Use in a drama situation. Choose other opposite feelings such as brave/scared, asleep/awake or angry/calm. (EAD2)

Activity: Can you find the opposite?

Learning opportunity: Playing a collaborative game to introduce opposites.

Early Learning Goal: Personal, Social and Emotional Development. Making relationships.

Resources: *Opposites* by Eric Carle; a selection of pairs of opposites such as old/new shoes, big/small balls, empty/full bottles, tall/short candles, black/white boxes, happy/sad faces, heavy/light bags; a bean bag.

Organisation: Whole group.

Key vocabulary: Opposite words, pairs.

What to do: Sit in a circle with the opposite pairs mixed up in the middle. Show the children the big ball and ask if anyone can show you the small ball.

Look at the big and small balls together and explain that they are 'opposite' to each other. Can the children show you any other opposites?

Read *Opposites* by Eric Carle or any other books about opposites. Teach the children this simple song (tune: 'London Bridge'):

Can you find the opposite, opposite, opposite?
Can you find the opposite of _____?

Choose one item from the centre of the circle, such as the old shoe. Ask them if it is old or new? Pass the beanbag around the circle as you sing the song. Whoever is holding it when the song ends must find the 'new' shoe to make a pair. Give each child a turn.

The final song:

We have found the opposites, opposites, opposites.
We have found the opposites, and now it's time to stop!

Activity: Happy/sad mobiles

Learning opportunity: Working imaginatively with a malleable material.

Early Learning Goal: Physical Development. Moving and handling.

Resources: A quantity of salt dough made using 2 cups of plain flour, 1 cup of water, 1 cup of salt, 1 tbsp oil; rolling pins; different-sized round cutters; brushes; paint; straws; string or ribbon; plastic hoop or metal coat hanger.

Organisation: Small group.

Key vocabulary: Circle, cutter, face, happy, smile, sad, tears.

What to do: Work with a small group of children to measure and mix the salt dough. Explain that it is not edible!

Give children time to experiment with the dough. Show them how to roll it out, not too thin, and cut out different-sized circles. Help them to make a small hole near the edge of each circle using a straw.

Talk about happy and sad faces. These can be painted later or made by punching out small circles for eyes and adding mouths made from thin sausages of dough in a happy or sad shape. Use a damp brush to join pieces of dough together.

Bake the dough very slowly in a cool oven, preferably overnight. The children can paint the faces on both sides. Help them to thread various lengths of ribbon through the holes and hang faces from the hoop. Display where visitors can see them.

Display

Paint two giant faces, one with a happy smile and the other looking sad, and display them on the wall. Mount the children's happy/sad photographs and self-portraits underneath.

Make a puppet theatre from a big cardboard box. Use drapes to make curtains. Place on a table and encourage children to perform puppet shows using the pop-up puppets and other finger or glove puppets.

Theme 2: Big and small

Communication and Language
- Read *Can't you Sleep, Little Bear?* by Martin Waddell. Create a bear cave in the role-play area (see activity opposite). (CL1, 3)
- Make a collection of size opposites such as long/short, fat/thin, narrow/wide and heavy/light. Scribe them on suitable shaped cards. (CL1, 2)

Physical Development
- Bring in a big bear and a small bear with a collection of different-sized clothes for the children to dress. Can they fasten the buttons or zips? (PD1, 2)
- Ask children to move around the room taking big steps in time to a steady beat on the drum. Then try little running steps in time to a faster beat. (PD1)
- Use play dough or clay to make long and short snakes. Measure the longest and shortest? (PD1)
- Play with big hoops and small quoits, and big and small balls. (PD1)
- Work together as a group to make a house, vehicle or rocket out of a large cardboard box. Use small match boxes or film canisters to make keepsake or treasure boxes (PD1)

Personal, Social and Emotional Development
- Read *Where's my Teddy?* by Jez Alborough. Talk about how big some things might look to small children. How would they feel if they met a real life-size bear? (PSE1, 2)
- Provide lots of different-sized clothes – some baby clothes, some adult-size, some child sized. Let the children have fun trying on the clothes. Can they find ones to fit properly? (PSE1, 3)
- Go on an opposites hunt looking for big and small things. Make a list of how many other opposites you spot. Don't forget to listen as well as look! (PSE1, 2)

Literacy
- Point out differences between some big (capital) and small letters. Help children to write their names on pre-cut circles using a capital letter at the beginning. Join letters into a name string and display. (L2)
- Practise writing letters and words on big pieces of paper using fat felt pens. Contrast with tiny words on small pieces of paper using thin felt pens. (L2)

Mathematics
- Use threading beads to make a big, small, big, small pattern. Ask children to make up their own repeating patterns. (M2)

- Use different-sized hands as non-standard measures (see activity opposite). (M1, 2)
- Fill same-sized boxes with different materials. Help children to estimate weight and put them in order (lightest to heaviest). Check results using scales. (M2)
- Explore the opposites 'empty' and 'full' using different-sized containers in the water and sand trays. How many small cups or spoons does it take to fill a bottle? Ask them to half-fill a bucket. Is it half full or half empty? (M1)

Understanding the World
- Invite children to use magnifying glasses to observe small things around the setting, inside and outside. Talk about how they make things look bigger. (UW2)
- Use different-sized construction toys to make big and small model vehicles. How do the models work? (UW2)

Expressive Arts and Design
- Work in groups to paint big pictures. Use big brushes big pots of paint and a huge canvas. Contrast this with using tiny pieces of paper, small brushes and paint trays. (EAD1)
- Enjoy acting out the story, singing and adding instruments to 'The Enormous Turnip' from *Three Singing Pigs* (see Resources). (EAD2)

Activity: Big bear, little bear

Learning opportunity: Using the role-play area to develop imaginative language and understanding of opposite words.

Early Learning Goal: Communication and Language. Listening and attention. Speaking.

Resources: *Can't You Sleep, Little Bear?* by Martin Waddell (Walker); a role-play area set out as a bear cave with dark area covered in blankets, big and small cups and plates, bedding, big chair, rug, toys; different-sized boxes; yellow Cellophane; red/yellow/orange collage materials; black paper; silver foil; a teddy bear.

Organisation: Whole group.

Key vocabulary: Big, little, dark, light, sleep, lantern.

What to do: Read the story to the children. Point out the opposites – big and little, light and dark.

Talk about creating a 'Bear cave' in the role-play area. Explain that you need to make a dark area by covering the climbing frame or corner with a blanket. Put a small duvet or bed in the dark area for Little Bear and a big comfy chair in the light area.

Make a fire for the light area using collage materials. Help children to make different-sized lanterns by cutting windows out of boxes and adding yellow Cellophane.

Encourage children to take it in turns to role play and retell the story using the dark and light areas and the different-sized lanterns. They could use a teddy bear for Little Bear. To make the 'biggest light of all' try covering the wall outside the cave with dark backing paper and sticking on stars and a giant silver moon made from silver foil.

Activity: Who has the biggest hands?

Learning opportunity: Exploring comparative size and measurement.

Early Learning Goal: Mathematics. Shape, space and measures.

Resources: Hands; paper; pencils; paint; rulers.

Organisation: Small group.

Key vocabulary: Measure, bigger, smaller, biggest, smallest, hand spans.

What to do: Help children to draw round their own hands and measure the length with a ruler.

Draw round some adult hands. Who has the biggest/smallest hands?

Use paint to make handprints and, starting with the biggest, print them in order of size.

Show children how to stretch their hands into a hand span. Measure this using a ruler. Explain that the children can use their hand spans to measure the lengths of objects in the room.

Ask children to work in pairs to measure different items such as width of table, height of cupboard, length of pencil or book, and of course each other.

Display

Place the construction model vehicles on a road layout and produce name labels on a computer.

Display printed hands in strips as a border around the room.

Make giant gold frames for the 'big' paintings using pasta and spray paint.

Ask children to design frames for the 'small' paintings using tiny dots and patterns.

Theme 3: Old and new

Communication and Language
- Read *Old Bear* by Jane Hissey (see activity opposite). (CL3)
- Play a cumulative circle game – 'I went to the shop and bought a new _____'. (CL2, 3)
- Read *A New Room for William* by Sally Grindley. Help children to work in pairs to draw and label their own design for a new room. (CL1, 2)
- Invite grandparents to share favourite stories and books with the children on 'Grandparent's Day.' (see PSED) (CL1)

Physical Development
- Help the children to carefully pack up the home corner into large cardboard boxes and move to a new house in another area of the setting. How could they make the new house different? (PD1)
- Play some old movement games such as 'Grandmother's footsteps', 'Farmers in his den' and 'Ring a ring of roses'. (PD1)
- On Grandparent's Day, invite the grandparents to demonstrate to the children some old traditional games such as marbles, jacks and tiddley winks. (see PSED) (PD1)

Personal, Social and Emotional Development
- During circle time, show children a collection of old and new objects. Can they sort them into two groups? How are they different? (PSE1, 2)
- Organise a Grandparent's Day. Invite grandparents or elderly neighbours to visit the setting. Make special food for the visitors and learn some games and songs to play on the day. (PSE1, 3)
- Read *Baggy Brown and the Royal Baby* by Mick Inkpen. Talk about old and best-loved toys. Invite the children to talk about their favourite, old, special toy. (PSE1, 2)

Literacy
- Write their own concertina book of the Old Bear story (see activity opposite). (L2)
- Write invitations for Grandparent's Day. (L2)
- Ask grandparents to bring in something old and special to show the children such as a photo, book, game or toy. Help children to write labels for the special items. (L2)

Mathematics
- Talk about how old the children are now. How old will they be on their next birthday? Make a chart to show the different birthdays in the group. Which month has the most birthdays? (M1)
- Draw a sheet with ten birthday cakes numbered one to ten. Or use playdough and make ten little cakes. Give the children coloured matchsticks. Can they draw or stick the correct number of candles on each cake? Adapt the rhyme 'Five little candles' from *This Little Puffin*. (M1)
- Sing this song to the tune of 'Hickory Dickory Dock':
  Is it your birthday today? x2
  How old are you? x2
  You are _____ today. (M1)
- Use a large model clock to introduce o'clock times. (M1)

Understanding the World
- Bake some fresh scones to share with the visitors on Grandparent's Day. Provide jam and cream. (UW2)
- Look at old photos of children playing. Talk about the clothes, toys, games and other things that have changed. Encourage children to see differences between past and present. Use a 'then and now' writing frame to help the children to record their ideas about old and new things. (UW1)
- Talk about memories and draw a family tree (see activity opposite). (UW1)

Expressive Arts and Design
- Design and make a card to send to a new baby. (EAD1)
- Learn this rhyme and have fun acting it out:
  Comfy shoes, old shoes,
  Hole in the toe shoes,
  Shiny shoes, new shoes,
  Sparkling clean party shoes.
  Which ones will you choose? (EAD1)
- Draw observational sketches of old and new objects (see PSED) using chalks and pastels on black and white paper. (EAD1)

Activity: Old Bear

Learning opportunity: Talking, role playing and retelling story using words and pictures.

Early Learning Goal: Communication and Language. Speaking. Literacy. Writing.

Resources: *Old Bear* by Jane Hissey; large sack or box; an old teddy bear; wooden bricks; soft toys; paper plant made from plastic flowerpot and green crepe paper; wooden aeroplane; handkerchiefs or squares of material with string tied on each corner; blanket; white paper folded into concertinas; pencils; felt pens.

Organisation: Whole group for story, small groups to use story sack and writing activity.

Key vocabulary: Old, new, vocabulary from book.

What to do: Read the story to the children. Why do they think Old Bear was put in the attic?

Talk about all the different ways the toys tried to rescue Old Bear. Act out some of these with the children such as building a tower out of bricks, and making a tower of soft toys. What happened to all these attempts? How did Old Bear get down safely in the end?

Put together a story sack or box with props (see Resources list) so that the children can act out the story in small groups. Use a tablet to film scenes and watch back with the rest of the group.

Ask children to make their own concertina books of the story by retelling the sequence of events using words and pictures. Help them to write a short sentence for each picture. Encourage children to show their stories to the group.

Activity: Family trees

Learning opportunity: Talking and finding out about children's memories and families.

Early Learning Goal: Understanding the World. People and communities.

Resources: *Me and My Family Tree* by Joan Sweeny; *The Memory String* by Eve Bunting; *My Grandma is Wonderful* by Nick Butterworth; paper; pencils; felt pens; photographs or drawings of the children.

Organisation: Whole group for introduction, small groups for recording activity.

Key vocabulary: Old, new, memories, remember, family tree.

What to do: Read a book about families or memories to the children.

Recall any memories that the grandparents may have shared with the children on Grandparent's Day. What can the children remember about when they were smaller?

Collect these memories, write them on pieces of paper and display them on the wall under the title 'We can remember'.

Help children to think of the names of people in their family, including grandparents, parents and siblings. Be sensitive to children who come from unconventional families.

Invite children to draw or stick a photograph of themselves in the middle of a piece of paper. Help them to add the names and draw pictures of their family around the paper to make a simple family tree.

Display

Put old and new items (see PSED) on an interactive display table so children can observe and handle them.

Mount and display photos from Grandparent's Day.

Display new baby cards and make photocopies of the best design to sell to parents to raise funds.

Paint a big bare brown tree shape and mount and display children's family trees on the branches.

Theme 4: Hot and cold

Communication and Language
- Set up two role-play corners in the room, one for hot weather with beach towels, sunglasses, sun hats, ice creams and buckets and spades, and the other for cold weather, with hats, scarves, gloves and hot buttered toast. (CL2, 3)
- Talk about what children like to do when it is hot or cold. Invite them to act out different activities for others to guess. (CL1, 2)

Physical Development
- Ask for a volunteer to leave the room while you hide a toy. Help them to find the hiding place by shouting 'hot' when they are near and 'cold' when they are far away. (PD1)
- Try some warm-up exercises to music. What happens to the children's bodies when they are warm? (PD2)
- Use white play dough made with cornflour to make models of animals that live in the snow. Display them on a black sugar paper background. (PD1)

Personal, Social and Emotional Development
- Talk about hot and cold weather. Look at pictures of life in hot and cold countries. Why are the clothes and houses so different? What do children wear in this country when it is hot or cold? (PSE1, 2)
- During circle time invite adults to come and talk to the children about visiting or living in hot or cold countries. (PSE3)
- Share hot and cold snacks. Try hot soup on a cold day and ice lollies on a hot day. Dip hot chips into cold tomato sauce. (PSE1, 3)

Literacy
- Use a writing frame to help record ideas for activities in hot and cold weather. Complete the sentence 'When it is hot I like to...'. (L2)
- Write a group poem entitled 'What is hot?' Collect lots of 'hot' words to use in the poem such as 'fire', 'sun', 'flames', 'red', and so on. Let children red pens to write the 'hot' words. Mount the poems on hot coloured paper. Then write a matching poem using cold' words. (L2)
- Make a collection of words that begin with the same initial sounds as hot and cold. Make up funny phrases by putting hot or cold in front of other words such as 'hot hat' and 'cold carrots'. (L1)

Mathematics
- Make hot and cold drinks for snack time. Use hot water to make hot chocolate and cold water to make orange squash. Draw a chart to show how many children chose each drink. (M1)
- Draw a hat, scarf and gloves and ask children to design a repeating pattern to make matching sets. (M2)

Understanding the World
- Experiment with ice. Help children to make coloured ice cubes using food colouring. How long does the water take to change into ice? Use vocabulary to describe change – liquid, solid, frozen, and so on. Take three shallow trays and fill one with hand-hot water, one with cold water and one empty. Place an ice cube in each tray. Which ice cube will melt first? (UW2)
- Make jelly with the children (see activity opposite). (UW2)
- Use a forehead thermometer strip to take children's temperatures. What happens if our temperature is higher than normal? (UW2)

Expressive Arts and Design
- Talk about 'hot' colours such as red and orange, and 'cold' colours such as blue and green. Ask children to create hot or cold collages using coloured paper, materials, paint and so on. (EAD2)
- Paint with ice cubes and powder paint. (EAD1)
- Make weaving frames out of polystyrene trays. Thread wool across. Provide a selection of red or blue weaving materials such as ribbon, strips of paper, foil and different fabrics. (EAD1)

- Design clothes for different temperatures (see second activity below). (EAD1)

Activity: Making jelly

Learning opportunity: Observing changes in materials using all the senses.

Early Learning Goal: Understanding the World. The world.

Resources: Jelly; measuring jug; water; fridge; jelly mould; bowls; spoons.

Organisation: Small group.

Key vocabulary: Hot, cold, melt, liquid, set, solid.

What to do: Explain that you are going to make jelly using hot and cold water.

Help children to wash their hands carefully.

Ask children to tear a block of jelly into cubes. What does the jelly smell of? What does it feel like?

Boil a kettle. Point out the steam coming from the kettle as the water boils. Dissolve the jelly in 280ml (half pint) of boiling water. What happens to the jelly as they stir it? Add another 280ml of cold water. Pour the jelly into a mould or an ice cube tray and put it in the fridge.

Talk to the children about what they think will happen to the jelly in the fridge.

Check after one hour to see if it has set, or leave overnight. Encourage children to notice how it has changed. Run the mould under warm water and turn onto a plate.

Serve jelly with cold ice cream and hot chocolate sauce for a treat!

Activity: What shall I wear...?

Learning opportunity: Working together to design clothes for all weathers.

Early Learning Goal: Expressive Arts and Design. Using media and materials.

Resources: Copy of 'What is the weather today?' from *Bobby Shaftoe, Clap your Hands* by Sue Nicholls; two large pieces of card; collage materials; paint.

Organisation: Two small groups.

Key vocabulary: Hot, cold, weather, clothes, temperature.

What to do: Sing 'What is the weather today?' (see Resources).

Help children to look outside and think about today's weather. Is it hot or cold outside? Talk about suitable clothes to wear in different sorts of weather (refer to hot/cold role-play areas).

Ask for two volunteers to lie down on a piece of card and be drawn around. Ask one group to design clothes for a hot day and the other for a cold day. Use paint for the faces and bodies and different materials for the clothes. Try to find woollen material for warm jumpers and lycra for swimming trunks, and so on.

Display the two dressed characters in the nursery labelled appropriately – 'Today is hot/cold'.

Display

Make a hot and cold patchwork quilt using contrasting squares or shapes cut from collages, paintings and weaving.

Help children to make a table display of a hot or cold country of their choice using books, maps, photographs, paintings, drawings, plastic animals and artefacts.

Theme 5: Loud and quiet

Communication and Language
- Read *Peace at Last* by Jill Murphy. Help children to add sound effects using voices, body percussion and/or instruments. Make a picture score of all the sounds the children use. (CL1, 2, 3)
- Ask children to make up stories about imaginary characters called Loud Luke and Quiet Queenie. Can they act out the adventures? (CL1, 3)

Physical Development
- Play 'As quiet as a mouse'. Pass a tambourine around the circle without making any sound at all. (PD1)
- Play 'Keeper of the bells'. Choose one child to be blindfolded in the center of the circle. Ask another child to try to creep up and steal the bells without waking the 'keeper'. (PD1)
- Opposites Dance: ask children to move around the room reacting to loud/quiet sounds on a percussion instrument. Try fast/slow and high/low sounds. Organise children into two groups and make the opposite movements at the same time. (PD1)

Personal, Social and Emotional Development
- Introduce the opposite words 'loud' and 'quiet'. Ask children to whisper or shout in response to your questions. 'Have you brought your quiet voice?' 'Yes I have, yes I have'. Have they brought any other contrasting voices? (PSE1, 2)
- Play 'Chinese whispers'. (PSE1, 3)
- Read *The Very Noisy Night* by Diana Hendry. Talk about how sounds can be scarey at night. What do the children do when they can't sleep? (PSE2)

Literacy
- Write a list of loud and quiet sounds under the headings 'as loud as an elephant' and 'as quiet as a mouse'. (L2)
- Write up the stories about Loud Luke and Quiet Queenie in concertina books with illustrations. (L2)

Mathematics
- Write patterns of loud and quiet sounds. Invent suitable symbols for loud and quiet. Ask children to write patterns of eight sounds for others to follow. Choose two instruments or vocal sounds and listen to the patterns. Can the listeners count how many loud or quiet sounds were made? (M1)
- Use instruments and dice to explore musical opposites (see activity opposite). (M1)

Understanding the World
- Investigate which instrument can make the quietest or loudest sound. Talk about what the instruments are made of. (UW2)
- Make shakers using empty cocoa or crisp tins (with metal base) filled with sugar, dried rice or beans. Which ones make a quieter sound and why? Try this rhyme:
  Shake the sugar, shake the sugar,
  Ssssh, ssssh, ssssh, ssssh!
  Bouncing beans, bouncing beans,
  Brrm, brrm, brrm, brrm! (UW2)

Expressive Arts and Design
- Explore conducting (see activity opposite). (EAD1)
- Make loud and quiet sounds on an instrument. Sit in a circle and ask children to react to the sounds, for instance, put hands on head (loud) and finger on lips (quiet). Ask children to close their eyes and move in response to the sounds. Invite children to play sounds for the group to move to. (EAD1)
- Enjoy making quiet 'night' and loud 'day' music for the Elves and the Shoemaker' from *Three Singing Pigs*. (EAD2)
- Listen to different examples of loud and quiet recorded music. Ask children to paint loud and quiet pictures as they listen. (EAD2)

Activity: Dice music

Learning opportunity: Reading numbers and rolling dice to select contrasting sounds.

Early Learning Goal: Mathematics. Numbers.

Resources: Six different musical instruments; one dice with numbers one to six; one dice with words – loud, quiet, fast, slow, long, short; paper; pencils.

Organisation: Small group.

Key vocabulary: Numbers one to six, loud, quiet, fast, slow, long, short.

What to do: Show the children the six different musical instruments and allow time for them to explore the sounds they can make. Label the instruments one to six. Help children to write a sequence of numbers for each other to play.

Introduce the game element by using dice. Children take turns to roll the number die and play the instrument that matches the number. They can roll the number die again to find out how many times to make a sound.

Show the children the word 'dice' and talk about musical opposites. Explain to the children that this die tells them how to play the instrument. Ask them to roll both dice. If the dice say '2' and 'quiet', they must play the instrument labelled '2' quietly and so on.

Activity: Conducting opposites

Learning opportunity: Working together to organise and make musical sounds.

Early Learning Goal: Expressive Arts and Design. Exploring and using media and materials.

Resources: A percussion instrument for each child.
Organisation: Whole group.

Key vocabulary: Start, stop, palms up, fists down, loud, quiet.

What to do: Sit in a circle and give everyone a percussion instrument or sound source. Place them in front of each child and ask them not to touch until they are asked to by the conductor.

Begin by playing the role of the conductor yourself. Stand in the middle of the circle and demonstrate two hand signals to the children – open palms up means start, closed fists down means stop. Ask all children to copy these hand movements. Encourage children to follow the conductor and start and stop playing their instruments. Ask for individuals to conduct the group.

Once they have grasped this, show the children how to adapt the signals to make the music change from loud to quiet. When the conductor's hands are far apart the music should be loud. If the conductor's hands are close together, the musicians should play quietly. Try conducting the whole group, small groups of similar instruments, or soloists.

Display

Paint a huge elephant and a tiny mouse to illustrate the loud and quiet word lists. Ask children to paint or draw pictures of Loud Luke and Quiet Queenie. Compile their stories into a book and display.

Make an interactive display of loud and quiet sounds inside identical containers such as variety cereal boxes or opaque plastic bottles using different fillings (beans, rice, sugar, sand, feathers, coins). Ask children to arrange in order of quietest to loudest sounds.

Theme 6: Up and down

Communication and Language
- Make a list of things that go up and down and write them on an open umbrella shape to display in your setting. (CL1, 2)
- Give four or five children a card each showing a different character (picture and word) such as Ursula Up and Danny Down. Make up a story using the characters. Ask children to stand up every time their character is mentioned and then sit down again. Try adding actions for each of the characters. (CL1, 2)

Physical Development
- Play 'Changes' (see activity opposite). (PD1)
- Borrow a small trampoline. Encourage children to take turns jumping up and down. Alternatively, step up and down onto a box. Who can keep going the longest? Take care to follow safety precautions. (PD1)
- Pretend to be 'Jack in the boxes'. (PD1)

Personal, Social and Emotional Development
- Talk about the 'Pyjama Party' and/or 'Opposites Parade' that will take place this week. What preparations do the children need to make? Discuss refreshments, clothes and so on. (PSE1, 3)
- Play some parachute games (see activity opposite). (PSE1, 3)
- Play 'Snakes and ladders'. Talk about the rules of the game. How does it feel to climb up the ladder or slide down the snake? (PSE2)

Literacy
- Design posters for the 'Pyjama Party'. Use words and pictures to share information with parents and carers. (L2)
- Write invitations to the 'Pyjama Party'. (L2)
- Make up their own stories using the Up and Down characters (see CL) for the group to listen to. Write and illustrate as a concertina book. (L1, 2)
- Sing the nursery rhyme 'Hickory Dickory Dock'. Ask children to draw a sequence of pictures to retell the nursery rhyme and label them with the words 'up' and 'down'. (L1, 2)

Mathematics
- Make a collection of other positional opposites such as in/out, front/behind, above/below, upstairs/downstairs, and so on. Ask children to hide a small toy or counter and then describe where it is using this language. (M2)
- Sing 'The rides at the fair go up and down' to the tune of 'The wheels on the bus'. Add actions and extra verses: 'One boy at the fair...', 'Two girls at the fair...', 'Three teddies...', 'Four cats...', and 'Five pigs...'. (M1)

Understanding the World
- Explore floating and sinking. Make a collection of items that will either float (stay up) or sink (go down) in water. Ask children to work in pairs. Can they find two things that float and two things that sink? (UW2)
- Make boats from off-cuts of soft wood, straws, nails, card and bottle tops. Do they all float? What makes them sink? (UW2)
- Have fun building up tall towers. What happens when they got knocked over? (UW2)

Expressive Arts and Design
- Sing 'the Grand Old Duke of York', 'Goosey, Goosey Gander' and 'Jack and Jill'. Help children to act out the rhymes. (EAD1)
- Cover the top and underside of a table with sugar paper. Ask children to paint decorations on the top and bottom of the table. Which is easier to do? Talk about famous artists who painted 'upside down' (such as Leonardo da Vinci). (EAD1, 2)

- Ask children to draw a simple up and down pattern onto a small polystyrene tile. Use rollers to cover the tile with printing ink. Press the tile face down on the paper. Make two or three repeated prints before adding more paint. (EAD1)

Activity: Parachute games

Learning opportunity: Playing a circle game with the parachute.

Early Learning Goal: Personal, Social and Emotional Development. Making relationships.

Resources: Small parachute or sari cut in half and sewn into a square; small balls; small teddies.

Organisation: Whole group.

Key vocabulary: Up, down, side, edge, balls, bounce, float.

What to do: Sit in a circle and ask children to hold onto a handle or the edge of the parachute or sari.

Gently make the parachute move up and down and chant 'up and down' as it moves. Try shaking the parachute and chant 'side to side'.

Place some small balls on the parachute and make them bounce up and down. Try singing (Tune: 'The wheels on the bus'):

The balls are bouncing up and down,
Up and down, up and down.
The balls are bouncing up and down,
As we sing.

Ask children to stand up and hold the edges of the parachute high up in the air. Can they make a ball fall through the hole in the centre of the cloth? Try bouncing teddies on the parachute and sing 'The teddies are jumping up and down' as before.

Activity: Changes

Learning opportunity: Changing level, speed and direction using large and small equipment.

Early Learning Goal: Physical Development. Moving and handling.

Resources: Large space; selection of large and small equipment such as climbing frame, slide, tunnels, balance beams, hoops, beanbags and so on.

Organisation: Whole group.

Key vocabulary: Up, down, fast, slow, over, under, forwards, backwards.

What to do: Explain to the children that they are going to play a game called 'Changes'. Ask children to stand in a circle and move around the room in a circle. When they hear one tap on the tambourine they have to change direction.

Practise this until children can respond quickly. Introduce another change – two taps means change speed (fast/slow), three taps means change level (high up/low down).

Set up a circuit of large and small equipment for the children to go round. Make sure there are lots of opportunities to go up and down slides, through tunnels, up climbing frames, jump up and down, climb in and out of hoops, and so on.

Try playing 'Changes' as they go round. Be sure to emphasise safety. Ask children to count how many circuits they can complete in five minutes. Use a stopwatch to time circuits. Who can complete the circuit in the fastest time?

Give out certificates to everyone who tries hard. Provide refreshments. You could use this as a sponsored fundraising event as part of the final week.

Display

Make a display of things that go up and down such as umbrellas, rockets, aeroplanes, birds, balloons, slides, and so on. Create a boat show in the water tray to display the children's model boats. Mount and display the children's press print pictures around the room.

Bringing it all together

'Pyjama Party'
Talk to the children about the 'Pyjama Party'. This could be a special session culminating in an 'Opposites Parade' during the last half hour to which parents, carers and friends can be invited. At the start of the topic, inform parents of the date of the special event and any help or resources you may need.

Preparation
Explain to the children that the 'Pyjama Party' will be a fun way to explore the opposites 'night' and 'day' and so enjoy doing 'night time' things during the day at nursery. Ask children to come to nursery wearing pyjamas, dressing gowns and slippers. The 'Opposites Parade' at the end will be an opportunity to show things that they have made during the topic and explain what they have learned to their families and friends.

Activities
Set up a variety of activities based on going to bed and night-time. Put teddy bears and dolls to bed in the home corner. Read bedtime stories and books about nocturnal animals. Talk about bath time, cleaning teeth and other bedtime routines. Sing bedtime songs and lullabies.

At snack time, sit in a circle on duvets, and share midnight snacks of hot chocolate and cookies. Ice happy and sad face biscuits to give out to the visitors at the parade. Make fruit kebabs with alternate pieces of different fruit. Make fruit cocktails using cold tea, lemonade, fruit juice, chopped fruit and ice. Serve with long and short straws in big and small cups.

Ask children to bring in torches labelled with their name. In a dark room, enjoy torch dancing to music. Help children to follow the beams of light from their torches as they dance around the room. Remember to have a stock of spare torches and batteries to avoid disappointments. If an overhead projector is available, make shadows and enjoy a shadow puppet show.

'Opposites Parade'
Help children in pairs to dress up or find objects to illustrate different opposites such as big/small, short/tall, fast/slow, high/low, hot/cold, new/old, happy/sad, good/bad, heavy/light, black/white, dirty/clean, and so on.

Show displays of children's work during the topic and teach songs and rhymes from previous weeks. Join in the 'Opposites Dance' from Theme 5 (Physical Development).

Play an 'Opposites' hunting game: collect pictures showing lots of opposite pairs. Cut up an old book or magazines. Hide one of each pair around the room, or outside. Give the remaining cards to groups of children and an adult. Can they find the missing pair?

Resources

All books were available from leading booksellers at the time of writing

Resources to collect
- Hand mirrors
- Opposite books, puzzles and games
- Camera
- Big and small teddy bears and clothes
- Magnifying glasses
- Old photographs of children
- Pictures of hot/cold climates
- Forehead thermometer
- Ice cube trays
- Parachute
- Trampoline.

Everyday resources
- Bottle lids, corks, tubes, wooden spoons, paper plates, polystyrene trays and large and small boxes for modelling
- Papers and cards of different weights, colours and textures, for example sugar paper, corrugated card, sticky paper, silver and shiny papers
- Dry powder paints for mixing, and mixed paints for covering large areas and printing
- Different-sized paintbrushes from household brushes and rollers to thin brushes for delicate work, and a variety of paint mixing containers
- A variety of drawing and colouring pencils, crayons, chalks, pastels and felt pens
- Salt dough ingredients and cutters
- Softwood, hammers, nails, lolly sticks, and bottle lids for woodwork
- CD player
- Percussion instruments.

Stories
- *Dogger* by Shirley Hughes
- *Where's my Teddy?* by Jez Alborough
- *Can't You Sleep, Little Bear?* by Martin Waddell
- *Happy Hippo, Angry Duck* by Sandra Boynton
- *Baggy Brown and the Royal Baby* by Mick Inkpen
- *Old Bear* by Jane Hissey
- *A New Room for William* by Sally Grindley
- *My Grandma is Wonderful* by Nick Butterworth
- *Me and My Family Tree* by Joan Sweeney
- *The Memory String* by Eve Bunting
- *The Very Noisy Night* by Diana Hendry
- *Peace at Last* by Jill Murphy
- *Outside Bears* by Sally Grindley
- *You and Me, Little Bear* by Martin Waddell
- *Big Brother, Little Brother* by Penny Dale
- *Happy! (A little Zeb book)* by Caroline Castle
- *What's Up Duck?* by Tad Hills.

Non-fiction
- *Opposites* by Sandra Boynton
- *Opposites* by Eric Carle
- *Animal Opposites* by Peter Horacek
- *Maisy Big, Maisy Small* by Lucy Cousins
- *Ways into History: Toys and Games* by Sally Hewitt
- *Old Hat New Hat* by Stan Berenstain
- *Now You Know Science: Hot and Cold* by Terry Jennings
- *Quiet LOUD* by Leslie Patricelli
- *Opposites* by Nick Butterworth.

Songs and rhymes
- *Bobby Shaftoe, Clap Your Hands* by Sue Nicholls
- *Three Tapping Teddies* by Kaye Umansky
- *This Little Puffin* by Elizabeth Matterson
- *High Low Dolly Pepper: Developing Music Skills with Young Children* by Veronica Clark
- *Three Singing Pigs* by Kaye Umansky
- *Bingo Lingo* by Helen MacGregor.

Resources for planning
- **England:** Statutory framework for the Early Years Foundation Stage (2012) (www.foundationyears.org.uk/early-years-foundation-stage-2012)
- **Northern Ireland:** CCEA (2011) 'Curricular Guidance for Pre-school Education' (www.rewardinglearning.org.uk/curriculum/pre_school/index.asp) CCEA (2006) Understanding the Foundation Stage (www.nicurriculum.org.uk/docs/foundation_stage/UF_web.pdf)
- **Scotland:** Learning and Teaching Scotland (2010) 'Pre-birth to Three: Positive Outcomes for Scotland's Children and Families' (www.ltscotland.org.uk/earlyyears/). The Scottish Government (2008) 'Curriculum for Excellence: Building the Curriculum 3 – A Framework for Learning and Teaching' (www.ltscotland.org.uk/buildingyourcurriculum/policycontext/btc/btc3.asp)
- **Wales:** Welsh Assembly (2008) 'Framework for Children's Learning for 3 to 7-year-olds in Wales' (http://wales.gov.uk/topics/educationandskills/schoolshome/curriculuminwales/arevisedcurriculumforwales/foundationphase/?lang=en).

Collecting evidence of children's learning

Monitoring children's development is an important task. Making a profile of children's achievements, strengths, capabilities interests and learning will help you to see progress and will draw attention to those who are having difficulties for some reason. If a child needs additional professional help, such as speech therapy, these cumulative profiles will provide valuable evidence.

Profiles should cover all the Areas of Learning, as defined by the relevant UK framework, and be the result of collaboration between practitioners, parents and carers. Parents should be made aware of your record keeping policies when their child joins your group. Show parents the types of documentation that you are keeping and make sure they understand their purpose. As a general rule, documentation should be open. Families should have access to their child's documentation at any time and know they can contribute to it. Take regular opportunities to talk to parents about children's progress. If you have formal discussions regarding children about whom you have particular concerns, a dated record of the main points should be kept.

Keeping it manageable

Documentation should be helpful in informing practitioners, adult helpers and parents and always be for the benefit of the child. The golden rule is to keep it simple, manageable and useful. Do not try to make records following every activity!

Documentation will basically fall into two categories – observations and reflections:

Observations

- **Spontaneous observations:** Sometimes you will want to make a note of observations as they happen e.g. a child is heard counting cars accurately during a play activity, or is seen to play collaboratively for the first time.

- **Planned observations:** Sometimes you will plan to make observations of children's developing skills within a planned activity. Using the learning opportunity identified for an activity will help you to make appropriate judgments about children's capabilities, strengths and interests, and to record them systematically.

To collect information:

- Talk to children about their activities and listen to their responses.
- Listen to children talking to each other.
- Observe children's work such as early writing, drawings, paintings and models. (Keeping photocopies or photographs can be useful in tracking progress. Photographs are particularly useful to monitor children's development in the outdoor environment.)

Sometimes it may be appropriate to set up 'one off' activities for the purposes of monitoring development. Some groups at the beginning of each term, for example, ask children to write their name and to make a drawing of themselves to record their progressing skills in both co-ordination and observation.

Reflections

It is useful to spend regular time reflecting on the children's progress. Aim to make some comments about each child each week, and discuss these regularly with colleagues and families.

Informing your planning

Collecting evidence about children's progress is time consuming and it is important that it is useful. When planning, use the information collected to help you to decide what learning opportunities you need to provide next for each child. For example, a child who has poor pencil or brush control will benefit from more play with dough or construction toys to build strength of muscles in the hands and fingers.

Example observation sheet

Name: Lucy Field

Date: 17.1.13

Area of Learning: Mathematics. Count reliably with numbers from 1 to 20.

Context (Please tick):

Child-initiated: √   Adult-led:
Alone: In a group: √

Observation: Lucy is playing outside with two friends. She is trying to build the tallest tower and counting the bricks. "1, 2, 3, 4, 5, 7, 8. Mine's 8. Yours is only 7." She knocks the tower down, chuckles and starts to build again, counting as she places the bricks. "1, 2, 3, 4, 5, 7." The tower falls over. "Oh blow. I wanted to do 20."

What next: Check Lucy knows 6 follows 5. Encourage use of the outdoor counting grids, skittles and number rhyme CD.

Observer: E. M. Hogg

Overview of areas covered through 'Opposites'

	Communication and Language	Physical Development	Personal, Social and Emotional Development	Literacy	Mathematics	Understanding the World	Expressive Arts and Design
Happy and sad	Listening and attention Understanding Speaking	Moving and handling Health and self-care	Self-confidence and self-awareness Managing feelings and behaviour Making relationships	Reading Writing	Numbers Shape, space and measures	People and communities The world Technology	Exploring and using media and materials Being imaginative
Big and small	Listening and attention Understanding Speaking	Moving and handling Health and self-care	Self-confidence and self-awareness Managing feelings and behaviour Making relationships	Reading Writing	Numbers Shape, space and measures	People and communities The world Technology	Exploring and using media and materials Being imaginative
Old and new	Listening and attention Understanding Speaking	Moving and handling Health and self-care	Self-confidence and self-awareness Managing feelings and behaviour Making relationships	Reading Writing	Numbers Shape, space and measures	People and communities The world Technology	Exploring and using media and materials Being imaginative
Hot and cold	Listening and attention Understanding Speaking	Moving and handling Health and self-care	Self-confidence and self-awareness Managing feelings and behaviour Making relationships	Reading Writing	Numbers Shape, space and measures	People and communities The world Technology	Exploring and using media and materials Being imaginative
Loud and quiet	Listening and attention Understanding Speaking	Moving and handling Health and self-care	Self-confidence and self-awareness Managing feelings and behaviour Making relationships	Reading Writing	Numbers Shape, space and measures	People and communities The world Technology	Exploring and using media and materials Being imaginative
Up and down	Listening and attention Understanding Speaking	Moving and handling Health and self-care	Self-confidence and self-awareness Managing feelings and behaviour Making relationships	Reading Writing	Numbers Shape, space and measures	People and communities The world Technology	Exploring and using media and materials Being imaginative

Note: For each theme, highlight the Early Learning Goal areas covered through both adult focused and child-initiated activities relating to 'Opposites'.

Home links

The theme of 'Opposites' lends itself to useful links with children's homes and families. Through working together children and adults gain respect for each other and build comfortable and confident relationships.

Establishing partnerships
- Keep parents informed about the topic of 'Opposites' and the activities for each theme. By understanding the work of the group, parents will enjoy the involvement of contributing ideas, time and resources.
- Photocopy the 'Family page' for each child to take home.
- Ask parents for help in inviting grandparents or elderly relatives or neighbours to your Grandparent's Day.
- Invite families, carers and friends to come to the special 'Opposites Parade' at the end of the topic.
- Invite parents to take photographs at the Grandparent's Day and the 'Opposites Parade'.

Visiting enthusiasts
- Invite adults who have lived in or visited hot/cold countries to visit the nursery and talk about their experiences. Make sure that visitors are well-briefed so that children's attention can be sustained.

Resource requests
- Invite parents to bring in old items for a hands-on display of machines, books, toys and photographs.
- Ask parents to help children find out about family members and their interesting life stories.
- Ask parents to bring in a photograph of their child to put on the family tree.

'Pyjama Party'
- Ask parents to encourage children to come to nursery in their pyjamas for the party.
- At the event, it may be helpful to have additional adults to help the children prepare and serve the refreshments, play games and take part in the 'Opposites Parade'.